Transplant

Prose and poetry by
Dave Olson

Copyright © 2019 *Transplant* by Dave Olson

All rights reserved. No part of this book may be reproduced without the express permission of the author, except in the case of brief excerpts embodied in critical articles and reviews.

Published by Piscataqua Press
an imprint of RiverRun Bookstore
32 Daniel Street
Portsmouth NH 03801

ISBN: 978-1-950381-23-4

Lessons & Memories

Santa Claus

They say that everyone goes through four stages of life in regard to Santa Claus. In the first stage you believe in him, next you grow mistrustful and don't believe, then you <u>are</u> Santa Claus, and finally you *look* like him. Although I am approaching the last stage, I have a few recollections of the first stage.

Our Santa Claus was benevolent, but aloof and spooky. When we were good (most of the time), he bestowed gifts—always under the Christmas tree and during the night when we couldn't see him. He must have read our minds because he was surprisingly good at leaving just what we wanted. However, he always left a few useful items like shoes, socks or mittens, too.

Each year our good behavior was assured by his visit to the house (always when Dad wasn't home!) where he would suddenly appear, pounding on the big window and scaring the hell out of my youngest brother and sister. After Mother calmed us down and got us to approach the window, he would rub his big belly, dance around the yard, wave and then he was gone into the darkness. When Dad returned, we were wide-eyed as we told him of the mysterious appearance and disappearance.

We then knew for sure that Santa was watching us. I never did understand how Santa could come down the chimney. Our chimney ended up in the basement in the coal bin! Why was he always seen outside, and with a clean white beard?

Brother Don and I entered the second stage the day we found the Santa Claus suit with clean white whiskers hidden under the icebox on the back porch. We were threatened and bribed into silence until Lloyd and Darielle were older. Santa didn't pound on the window anymore.

Cowboys and Indians

Like most kids of our generation, playing cowboys and Indians was one of our common activities, especially when the weather cooperated and we could yell and shoot and gallop our imaginary horses through the yards. However, the cowboy and Indian games I remember most were indoors on winter holidays.

On Christmas, New Years, and several other Sundays, the number of participants increased from four (the Olson kids) to seven thanks to the addition of Shirley, Marlene and John Grout – enough for several cowboys and several Indians. In the morning after greetings, exchanges of gifts and coffee and snacks, Dad and Uncle Jack would settle at the dining room table for some serious cribbage playing and Mother, Aunt Fedelia, and sometimes aunts Grace and Tootsie would get busy in the kitchen talking and preparing dinner. This left some open country (the living room and part of the dining room) for the cowboys and Indians.

The large overstuffed sofa (sometimes a mountain and sometimes a horse), hassock and easy chairs were parts of the western terrain. The dining room table in the adjacent room was also a mountain, but that was dangerous territory. Our trail for pursuing the Indians was a large figure eight around the sofa and the dining room table. The three girls made good Indians because when threatened, they screamed and ran so us cowboys could yell and give proper chase. The imaginary horses we were riding were often unsatisfactory for the chase. One day the four cowboys–Dave, Don, Lloyd and John–mounted the sofa horse all at once; it fell over backwards and the Indians escaped.

While the mothers and aunts were isolated from much of the clamor and noise, Dad and Jack had a more difficult time trying to concentrate on cribbage. Dad was not as fast with numbers and scores as Uncle Jack, who was an investment banker. Naturally, heated discussions ensued. Once in a while when our pursuit took us around the dining room table mountain, the long arm of justice would reach out to grab one of the tribe or the posse and leave him or her dangling in mid-air by the back of the shirt. We could never understand why justice could not distinguish between the "good cowboys" and the "bad Indians."

Saturday Night Baths

Some of my earliest childhood memories are Saturday night baths. Our upstairs bathroom was large and had a free standing cast iron bathtub with ornate legs. The house was heated with a coal-fired furnace and the hot air register was next to the tub. Us four little kids would line up naked and all try to stand over the hot air at once. Mother would wash and Dad would dry, the littlest child first and then the next and the next without changing the water. The rather unsatisfactory supply of hot water came from the coil in the furnace so hot water had to be conserved. After us kids were bathed and dressed and put to bed, Dad and then Mother would bathe – probably in the same water!

Pocket Goods

Except for photographs, I have relatively few physical things to remember Mother by. One is a small carving of a white tail deer fawn and the other a faded handmade potholder. Both have spent many hours in my pocket.

I was inspired by Walt Disney's first major animated movie, *Bambi*. Not by the message because I was already being introduced to the concept of hunting, but by the shape and the clean, smooth lines and coloration of the fawn Bambi. I found an end board from an orange crate and began carving and sanding and painting my own Bambi, which was later presented to Mother as a gift. After Mother's death, Dad had Bambi for a while, then Grandma Charlotte, then brother Lloyd and now my daughter Laurie. I see the Bambi carving, now more than 50 years old, now and again and remember my birth mother.

The other "thing" was a faded and crumpled, handmade, but never completed potholder. As an art class project in grade school, I decided to make Mother a potholder for a Christmas present. My teacher provided materials and instruction and I made the design and started to assemble it. Sewing never comes easy for a small boy, especially when trying to hide such a sissy activity from other boys. The unfinished potholder stayed in the pocket of my jeans for quite a while. One day my jeans got washed and Mother found the soggy, crumpled-up mess. I couldn't understand why she cried and cried about something I couldn't give her for Christmas. She kept the potholder and cherished it just the same.

Donut Day

Mother had a recipe for potato donuts which she had learned from Grandma Peterson. While we could always depend on finding some potato donuts at Grandma's, they never seemed to last at home, perhaps because the whole neighborhood knew about them.

On those special "donut days," Mother would make a big pan of dough and let it rise. The kitchen table would be covered with a cloth to roll out the dough and cut donuts. They were fried in a large black cast iron pot on the stove, but there was no room to cool them in the kitchen, so they were laid out on a table on the back porch. Thus, the aroma of freshly cooked warm donuts wafted through the air and the neighborhood children were drawn like bees to honey.

My brothers and sister and I were assigned the task of "watching" the donuts. Of course we had to sample them and then let our friends sample them too. That took care of the first batch, but soon the word got out and another wave of hungry kids would arrive. Mother made more donuts. By the time the donut frying was done, there were scarcely enough donuts for Dad's lunch box the next day.

Over the years the recipe was lost. Remembering the taste of fresh potato donuts, I still haunt the donut shops and ask my friends if they have ever tasted potato donuts. If you have the recipe, please send it to me.

King of the Marbles

Brother Don was the neighborhood marble shark. He won all the time and accumulated cans and boxes and bags of them — mine too! Once a game began, he never quit until he had all the marbles or it was too dark to play or the other boys were called home to supper. It was the same every spring when the winter turned warm and the ground was dry. Don and his favorite shooter would go out and clean up the neighborhood.

Don never did much with the marbles except keep them until Mother found a use for some of them. One of her favorite songs was "My Blue Heaven." When happy, she sang or hummed it around the house. After we got the cabin at Yellow Lake, she named it "Blue Heaven," but she needed a sign. When we built the steps of concrete for the back door, she selected the bluest of the marbles and she and Don pressed them into the wet cement to make the words.

Don had other entrepreneurial skills, some of which he taught to me. Each spring when strawberries were ripe, we rode our bicycles out to the small farms around Minneapolis. If we picked two crates for the farmer, we were allowed to pick one for ourselves. We each picked three crates and then strapped ours onto our bicycles and headed for home. On the way, we sold fresh strawberries door-to-door and seldom had any left for Mom.

A huge pile of rotten cow manure was a real gold mine for Don. He asked for and received permission to dig "some fishing worms" in it. Instead of fishing, Don made money. He kept the local bait shop supplied with large white grubs for two whole summers.

I believe Don learned his entrepreneurial skills early from Grandma Peterson, whom he stayed with and helped each summer when he was small. While I was in Grantsburg learning to be one of the "boys of summer," Don was raising his "own" flock of chicks or feeding his "own" calf or raising his "own" garden right next to Grandma's. Grandma Peterson certainly had to have entrepreneurial ability; she managed an 80-acre farm for about 30 years after Grandpa Peter died.

As he grew older, Don used his entrepreneurial skills to acquire a farm, a resort, a greenhouse, a florist business, and several apartments and houses.

The Beaver

Mose Vorm loved good times, good food, and surprises. One winter day he showed up for a visit in Minneapolis and presented Mother with a package that contained a large beaver all skinned and cleaned and ready for cooking. I could see the gleam in his eyes as well as his grin, and hear his chuckles as he enjoyed Mother's consternation at what she was supposed to do with a naked beaver that she was expected to cook!

Mose was an excellent chef and his resort, Ike Walton Lodge, on Yellow Lake was well known for the food, especially the game and fish that he and his wife Marie served. He assured Mother that the beaver would be delicious and then patiently guided her through the preparation and cooking, all the time enjoying her comments and reservations about cooking a "rodent." The aroma was wonderful and when it was served, it was huge, bigger than a turkey. Mose had also brought some apples for pie and some "skanky" cheddar cheese – to him, no meal was complete without apple pie and cheese for dessert.

What a feast! That beaver was the best meat I have ever eaten – sort of a cross between good roast venison and mallard duck. Mose watched, his eyes gleaming with satisfaction, as we enjoyed the meal and stuffed ourselves (even Mother). Then he took out his pocket knife, cut off a slice of cheese and ate his apple pie. Often when I have apple pie with cheese I think about Mose Vorm, his pocket knife and that wonderful roast beaver.

Guns to Grow Up With

As Dad began to take us hunting, he needed a gun to train us, but he couldn't afford a gun for each of his three sons. He solved this problem with one gun – a used single shot Iver Johnson 20-gauge shotgun with a full choke. The price was five dollars. To make it fit my brother Don, he cut two sections off the stock and covered it with a rubberized kick pad. As Don grew bigger, a section was screwed back on each year until he was big enough for a gun of his own; then I started with the 20-gauge. The gun was excellent for training because we conserved shells, the full choke taught us to shoot well, and the exposed hammer allowed Dad to check for safety at a glance.

There were no hunter safety courses in those days, but we each had to carry that gun empty for a full season of ducks, pheasants, and deer so that Dad could teach us proper gun handling and etiquette. Occasionally we could take a supervised shot at a stump or tin can. Infractions of the rules resulted in a whack on the ear or worse – shame before other hunters. That 20-gauge is still a hard-hitting gun. I killed seventeen ducks with it the first trip that I carried it loaded.

Dad's pride and joy was a .25 Remington automatic deer

rifle which he purchased for ten dollars. It had been sorely mishandled and was covered with rust. Dad spent many evenings at the kitchen table covered with newspapers bringing that gun back into shooting condition. It was completely disassembled and every part was carefully rubbed with steel wool until all the rust was gone and the action operated smoothly. The gun lost all its bluing and now has a silver grey patina. The cracked stock is glued together and wrapped in copper wire with silver solder. The butt is covered with a handsome laced leather kick pad. This fast, flat shooting rifle began earning its reputation as a deer slayer the first season that Dad used it and has accounted for dozens of deer over the years. Often it was passed from one hunter to the next as deer were bagged. All three of Dad's sons bagged deer with that rifle.

There are other guns with similar histories which we used as we grew up. None of these are valuable collector's items but each is precious and now owned and cherished by a son or grandson.

Deer Poachers

The pine barrens north of Grantsburg hardly supported the families that hung on there trying to wrest a living from the sterile sandy soils. The land should never have been divided up and sold for farming, but after the timber barons cut the timber, they burned the slash and then sold the 40-acre parcels to settlers. These hard-pressed families cut firewood and pulpwood, raised chickens, planted gardens, picked blueberries, and poached deer. Venison was a staple meat supply for these families year-round. As long as one hunted in the daylight and didn't use a spotlight at night, the neighbors didn't mind; they were all in the same boat. However, the game wardens did mind, and these dedicated public servants did their job admirably. Often they brought the culprit, the gun, and the dead deer to court in Grantsburg. The poachers invariably asked for a jury trial and were found not guilty. The jury always included merchants, bankers, and ministers from the local community. They knew that a guilty verdict meant that they would have to support the culprit in jail and his family on welfare and that the unpaid bills would remain unpaid.

The Canoe-Boat

With three growing boys who all wanted to go fishing, and the opportunity for family boat rides on Yellow Lake, Dad needed a boat, but there just wasn't money for that kind of luxury in the early forties. One day Dad came home with an old white decrepit canoe on top of his car. The city parks department was getting rid of old canoes and Dad bought one for ten dollars. It was an 18-foot cedar canvas-covered canoe with sponsons (special flotation chambers) on each side. The sponsons made it wider, less tippy and more seaworthy, but this craft didn't float – it needed extensive rebuilding.

Then there followed many evenings of work in the garage. The old canvas was removed and the broken and rotted cedar planking was replaced using special copper nails. The canoe and sponsons were re-canvassed and then the canoe was reassembled and treated with several coats of waterproof light green paint. I watched and helped wherever I could, often stretching the canvas with tools Dad had made for that task. Since Dad had three sons, the craft needed more seats. Dad made an extra seat near the middle and installed oar locks with short oars. He also made a motor bracket for the rear and varnished all the exposed wood. For the small investment (the new canvas cost more than the canoe) and Dad's skill and effort, we now had a "canoe-boat" that would hold three or four people safely and was a dream to row.

This craft provided many good days of fishing, hunting, and exploring for the family and for me when I used it alone. I even did some courting in it. Several times each summer I would row three miles across Yellow Lake to the extensive weed beds at the mouth of the river. Then I would put a large silver Doctor or KB Spoon on my line, brace the rod against my shoulder, and paddle the canoe-boat. The strikes were tremendous, sometimes tipping me back on the seat. The northern pike would then commence towing me and the canoe-boat around the lake. Because it was difficult for me to handle the boat and fight the fish, I never landed one larger than ten pounds. The really big ones would eventually get tired of my game and burrow down in the weeds until they were free and I was left with twenty or thirty pounds of weeds.

The trip with this canoe-boat that I remember best was fishing on Millacs Lake with Dad and my brother Don. The canoe-boat was then equipped with a 2½ HP Johnson motor and we were trolling for walleyes. After an hour or so, Dad located a large rocky underwater reef that was loaded with large 14-16 inch yellow perch and medium sized walleyes. We put out a marker and each pass by the marker yielded strikes and a fish or two. Eventually a commercial party boat with about ten sportsmen showed up and made a pass by our marker. I told Dad and he said it was alright – the water belonged to everyone. Next the party boat made a tight turn behind our boat and cut off our lines. Dad patiently reassembled our tackle and we began fishing again. Dad pulled up alongside the party boat and politely told the skipper he had turned a little too close and cut off our lines. Instead of an acknowledgment or apology, the skipper yelled and swore at Dad and said we shouldn't be out there fishing in that little boat. Dad told us to reel in our lines, that we had enough fish, and we were going home. Then he gunned the motor and turned right behind the party boat and cut off all ten lines! He pulled up alongside and told the red-faced skipper that perhaps he would now learn to respect other people's right to fish. As we went on our way, the skipper was cursing, but the sportsmen were smiling, cheering, and clapping.

Iced Crappies

On the occasional winter weekend trips to visit Grandmothers Peterson and Olson, Dad would take his boys ice fishing for crappies on Wood Lake.

The intense cold of northern Wisconsin usually provided ice thick enough to drive on and when there hadn't been any snow, it was Dad's turn to have some fun. As we drove on the ice to the fishing spot, Dad got the car going faster and faster, then hit the brakes and turned the wheel. The car would spin round and round while we hung on and screamed with excitement.

Once at "the spot," Dad would chop holes, each about two feet apart, in a semi-circle and sit on a box in the middle. His fishing rigs were homemade from the wooden handles of old golf clubs. Each had pegs on the side on which the thirty to forty feet of line, leader, and a hook were wound. A sharpened nail replaced the head of the club so that the fishing rig could be stuck into the ice alongside the hole. The thin pencil bobbers were adjusted to hold a small minnow about 20 inches off the bottom. Then we watched and waited – each boy assigned to two holes. When a crappie bit and the thin bobber began to slide below the water, Dad would grab the rod, set the hook and hand it to one of us ordering, "Run!" Run we would till the leader appeared and Dad flipped a crappie out on the ice. Dad would bait up again and feed the line down the hole as we returned with the rod. In this way we stayed warm and Dad concentrated on catching fish. The fun usually lasted until about two hours before dark.

After the crappies began to accumulate on the ice and freeze, I would put a layer of snow in the bottom of a wooden box and then a layer of frozen crappies and repeat the packing till the box was full. At home in Minneapolis, the crappies kept frozen most of the winter on our unheated back porch. When needed, I would dig the required number of fish out of snow, clean them and Mother would cook them for supper.

Footprints in Time

Some New England families have a tradition of leaving messages hidden in walls or other nooks and crannies in their houses, and barn builders often leave their names in several places as they build. These are messages for future occupants that say "We were here," or "I built this."

The Olson family didn't have to leave hidden messages at the cabin on Yellow Lake. Our messages were six footprints and six handprints in the concrete steps and walkways that we made. Pressing of the hands and feet in the fresh cement was a kind of reward ceremony after a hard day of mixing and pouring concrete.

In front of the cabin, the handprints are pressed into cement among the yellow and gold marbles from brother Don's collection. This area of steps and walkways is exposed to the sun and rain and now after 60 years the handprints are weathered and shallow but they are still there, all in a row, biggest to smallest, if you know where to look.

The footprints in the back of the cabin are in the shade back under the eaves out of the weather. They are fresh as the day they were made. As I look at them now, I can remember Mother sitting there trying to reshape her footprint to hide her flat foot about which she was very embarrassed. The massive concrete steps that contain these footprints include about a half ton of reinforcing steel, mostly used auto parts such as tie rods and steering columns from Dad's work. The footprints have been there more than 60 years and I believe they will be there long into the future. They are "footprints in time."

Never a New Car, Always a Good Car

The old story about the carpenter whose house is falling down or the plumber whose fixtures leak didn't apply to Dad. As a mechanic, he was a marvel at finding good, serviceable automobiles for his family and eventually for each of his three sons. These were never new cars, and often they had high mileage or were in their second or third ownerships, but they were safe and they ran and ran.

It was not surprising to see Dad come home from work in the evening with a different car that needed some mechanical repairs or body work. These were never new cars, but they were better than the one he had driven to work in the morning. After a few evenings of repairs and maybe some body work from a friend in exchange for Dad's work on a front end, our "newer" car was on the road.

For a growing family struggling to get by in the 30s and 40s, we were surprisingly mobile, and we had good cars. Most summer weekends we traveled to the cabin (100 miles one way) in Wisconsin and there were many trips to fish and hunt in the fall, winter, and spring. During gas rationing in World War II, the travel had to be carefully planned. To conserve gasoline, Dad would ride the trolley to work. I can still remember him carefully adding his weekly gas ration to the 55-gallon drum, which he kept (illegally) in the garage. He was a master at driving for fuel economy and he taught this skill to each of his sons as well.

One memorable accident occurred early in the morning on icy back roads as we met another car hurrying to go deer hunting. Rather than risk human injury from a side collision, Dad yelled, "Brace yourselves," and took a head-on hit. The other car had to be towed away. After making sure his passengers were all ok, and before the fluids had completely drained out of the broken radiator, Dad made plans to get his injured vehicle home. In order to keep our spirits up, he stayed surprisingly cheerful, and we built a fire and had coffee and stayed warm and comfortable. Poles and braces were cut in the woods to straighten the fenders and bumper, and the steering was adjusted. We made a bumper to bumper hitch to another car with a spare tire as a cushion, and towed our car home before dark the same day. It was my job to ride in the cold injured vehicle and turn the steering wheel as needed. We were back hunting again the next weekend.

Most men never forget their first car. Dad found mine for me – a 1935 Ford coupe with a rumble seat. What a dream for a young man! We scraped and sanded its old gray paint and Dad traded some work for a beautiful forest green paint job. I reupholstered the entire inside with ivory-colored leatherette material. Dad equipped me with a fuel pump, a starter, an ignition coil, a fan belt, and the proper tools for changing and repairing tires. I was king of the road! There were many happy miles and hours hunting, fishing, and entertaining girlfriends in that car. However, all good things come to end. The end for my coupe was a rear end collision by a drunk who ran into it while it was parked. Although drivable, the body work was too expensive to repair and the insurance company paid me more than I paid for the coupe. I kept driving it for a short while and later sold it – again for more than I paid for it. I miss that beautiful green coupe. I hope it is still running and I dream of having another just like it.

The Garbage Can

Behind our house in Minneapolis there was a narrow fifteen-foot wide concrete alleyway which provided access and service for the garages and backyards of all the houses on the block. Since the house lots were small, the garages were set close to the alleyway, and there was little visibility as well as a fifteen mile-an-hour speed limit.

Some of the neighbors, especially young drivers, didn't understand or care about the reduced visibility and the fifteen mile-an-hour speed limit. Dad was concerned for our safety. Occasionally when he was working in the garage in the evening, he would hear a car coming too fast. He would swear, drop his tools, and rush to the edge of the alley only to see the culprit speed past, ignoring his waving arms.

One evening Dad didn't work in the garage. Instead he laid an empty garbage can on its side out of sight behind the corner of the garage. Then he lit up a smoke, leaned against the garage and waited. After a while he heard the engine start and the tires squeal on the concrete as the young driver came tearing down the alley. Dad casually placed his foot on the garbage can and at just the right moment, gave it a kick. The terrified driver practically turned his car inside out to avoid a collision with the garbage can. Before he could come to his senses, Dad was at the side of the car and had the door open and the driver by the shirt collar. With steel in his eyes, he said, "That could have been my kid."

Needless to say there wasn't any more speeding in the alley.

The Swimming Hole

The swimming hole in Grantsburg's Wood River was a gathering place for naked boys in summer. Since the preferred sunny sand bank was across the deepest water, new boys had to pass an informal initiation by swimming across. No fair walking around; it was sink or swim to be "one of the boys." My first five or six strokes with random kicking seemed to take a lifetime and I knew the boys wouldn't pull me out till I was drowned. Eventually I could swim across, and then the downstream length of the deep water, and, finally, I could hold my own swimming against the current. I was one of the boys.

Most of our time was spent lying in the sun playing jack knives or "proving" our manliness by swearing, chewing, puffing, or inhaling; fortunately, I didn't get hooked. All new items were shared, including my new Packard bicycle. Each boy tried it out and had a naked ride up the path to within sight of downtown, then a quick turn, and a fast ride back to the bushes that hid the swimming hole.

One afternoon our peace and quiet was interrupted by the sound of giggling girls. (There is nothing more shameful than naked boys undergoing puberty and nothing more curious than girls just past that stage.) One quick glance revealed girls, a whole group of them, coming down the path. We all dove to the deepest part of the swimming hole and stood submerged and helpless in water up to our necks to be laughed at and ridiculed by these girls. Nothing, not even our most manly swearing and handfuls of wet sand and mud, would disperse them. Finally we took brave, concerted action and together we emerged, exposed our nakedness and ran after the girls, who took off screaming all the way back to town.

Our favorite time at the swimming hole came in late summer when the days were hot and sultry and we could eat watermelon. The river, now low, was full of sandbars and we could run for long distances, seldom having to get wet except to cool off. At the same time, we were completely hidden by the brushy banks. Occasionally we peeked out to look for watermelons which were sometimes grown on the fertile bottomland soils along the river. Most of the farmers expected nighttime raids along the roads, not brazen daytime thefts at the back of the fields by naked boys. Once in hand, the melons were dropped into the river to begin a leisurely float down to the swimming hole, where we waited to fish them out. Some got hung up in back waters or on sandbars and later came bobbing down the current at unexpected but welcome times.

Our swimming hole is now a marshy backwater flooded by the damming of Memory Lake, and Grantsburg has a supervised outdoor swimming pool constructed by the high school. I wonder if today's kids have as much fun as we did.

Two Black Gnats

When I first learned to cast a fly line, there was little extra money for flies. I only had two black gnats for a long time.

The cottage at Yellow Lake was located within a comfortable driving distance (i.e. 20 miles) for most of our relatives and in summer there were frequently a bunch of them for Sunday visits. Food for 15 or 20 people could be a problem, but most brought salad or dessert dishes and left the main course up to Mother and Dad. Economics dictated that it was either a dish like Hungarian goulash or fish. It was my job to provide the fish.

On many Saturday mornings in May, June, and July I was dropped off at Devils Lake – barefoot with my fly rod and a burlap bag attached to my belt. I waded out among the bulrushes and cast my two black gnats over the spawning beds of bluegill and pumpkinseed sunfish. They bit like crazy and I often caught two at a time. Gradually the burlap bag got heavier and heavier, but I didn't have to lift it because the fish in the bag swam or floated with me as I waded. After a couple of hours, my casting arm was very tired and sore from casting and catching fish. When Dad finally came to pick me up, I would be sitting in the shade resting my arm and watching my bag of fish which was too heavy to lift out of the water.

After lunch it was my job to clean the fish and prepare them for Sunday dinner. Since there were always 50 bluegills, sometimes as many as 100, it was a long afternoon of cleaning fish, but the two black gnats had done it again!

The Buck that Nearly Killed Me

Dad developed a safe efficient pattern for hunting deer while keeping track of his three sons. Before dawn we were in the woods on a well-known trail that allowed each of us to occupy a good stand. These stands were spaced out in a large loop and each of us knew where the others were sitting or standing and waiting for deer, i.e. "The Knob," "The Beer Keg," " The Preacher's Hand," "The Hollow Stump," "The River Crossing," etc. We were all carefully settled and quiet by dawn when other hunters entered the woods and began moving deer. In mid-morning we all moved to one stand to check on each other, have some coffee and settle down again. Soon the other hunters, hungry and tired, were heading for their cars and lunch and they moved the deer again. By mid-afternoon, the woods were quiet and we checked on each other again, began dragging deer and made plans for the evening hunt.

My buck, a nice eight-pointer, came by me one morning on the river crossing and my shot dropped him close to the river. When I got to him and looked him over, I discovered that it was the same deer I had hit in the lower rear leg the day before. After I got over the adrenalin shakes and had him dressed out, I sat on my stand and thought what a coincidence it was to get a shot at the same deer two days in a row and I wondered why. Was it just really good luck that I didn't have to remember leaving a wounded deer in the woods?

When Dad came by to check on me, we decided it would be easier to drag him down the river valley to the road rather than over the hills to the car. Since it was before noon, we thought I could get him out alone and I gave Dad my heavy clothes, thermos, and lunch, and kept my gun. I started dragging but I didn't get 200 yards before I knew that buck had come back to kill me from dragging him! He now seemed to weigh over 300 pounds. I decided to put him in the river and float him out. It was really easy. With his heavy coat of hollow deer hair, the buck floated and the water was only a couple feet deep. All I had to do was wade along and hold his antlers up. The water was near freezing and my feet were getting numb, but it was better than dragging. Then I hit the remains of an old beaver dam under the water and fell into the downstream deeper water. Instinctively I rolled over on my back so I could hold my gun above water. The buck's antlers caught in the beaver dam and his body swung in the current and stopped on top of me. I was trapped. That buck was still trying to kill me!

Somehow I managed to wiggle out from under him, but I had to get my gun wet as I used it for a brace to get up. The next hour and the half mile to the road were brutal. My clothes were saturated with near freezing water and I was numb with cold and shivering but I kept moving – glad to be alive!

That buck provided some of the strongest, toughest, worst-tasting venison I ever ate, but eat it I did. I felt he had it coming!

You Can't Take it With You

Among deer hunters it is said that each is entitled to one really good buck in a lifetime. Dad's buck came late in life when he was sixty-five.

After retirement, Dad and Charlotte often hunted together. They would get up early, bundle up with warm clothes, and carry their lunch and thermos of hot coffee into the woods. They would sit quietly back-to-back and watch for deer for hours at a time. Dad always wore his red wool tie because he believed it was good luck to get dressed up for the deer.

One day, Charlotte and Dad were sitting on their favorite spot off the end of Walls' field when Dad got a shot at a running deer. Charlotte was surprised and startled and said, "That shot was awfully close." Dad said, "It was me and I got a deer!" When they got to the deer, they found a magnificent 10-point buck with especially tall tines on its antlers. Shortly, a group of tired, red-faced hunters showed up. They had been chasing that buck all morning and were very angry that Dad had bagged it. This huge buck was much too heavy for Dad and Charlotte to drag, but Dad didn't dare ask for help lest they steal his deer. When they finally left, Dad had Charlotte sit right on the deer and hold his rifle in case they came back again.

Dad got his old hunting car and drove it right through the woods, knocking down clumps of brush and small trees till he got to the deer. The buck was too heavy for them to lift, so they scavenged around for pieces of rotten logs and clumps of sod and stuffed them under first one end of the deer and then the other. Thus they gradually built a mound under the deer until it was up high enough to push into the trunk of the car. It didn't push easily so Dad crawled into the trunk and pulled while Charlotte pushed. The buck went in right on top of Dad and he was trapped! After considerable swearing and yelling and more pushing and pulling, he managed to extract himself from below the buck. Triumphantly, the two 65-year-old hunters drove off with the best deer Dad had ever bagged.

The deer stayed in the trunk for a while so Dad could show it off to friends, relatives, sports at the local bars and the bowling alley and the deer check station. Later Dad mounted the antlers on a wooden plaque and hung them in a prominent spot in the living room. He showed the antlers to anyone and everyone who came by and regaled everyone with the story of his big buck. Naturally, the story was somewhat embellished, but who would question the veracity of a senior citizen? As he grew older, Dad's memory began to slip but he remembered the story of his big buck. Trouble is he didn't remember that he had told it just fifteen minutes before. Needless to say, his love of brandy didn't do anything but make that situation worse.

One day brother Lloyd and Dad were playing golf and Dad was celebrating the completion of each hole with a drink of brandy. Between the brandy and the repeated accounts of his big buck, Dad was also minimizing his strokes. Lloyd was frustrated and having a problem keeping track so that he could drop enough of his own strokes to stay even. Halfway through the sixth repetition of the big buck story Lloyd had had enough and said, "That damn buck! I'm sick and tired of hearing about it. When you die I'm going to bury those antlers with you!" Dad stopped and smiled and said,

"You know, I'd like that."

When Dad finally passed away at 79, Lloyd was first on the scene to console Charlotte, help with funeral arrangements, and share her grief. As Lloyd was trying to adjust to the now somewhat empty house without Dad, he happened to notice the antlers of Dad's big buck still proudly displayed on the wall. He told Charlotte about the day on the golf course. She got his red wool tie and said, "This belongs with the antlers."

Together they took the antlers and tie to the undertaker and asked if he could do it. The undertaker, a deer hunter himself, admired the beautiful antlers and said, "Let's see if they fit." They did and Dad's body was buried with the buck's antlers and his tie around his feet. This was to be a special family secret, but a story like that in a small northern Wisconsin town full of deer hunters had to get out. The undertaker told the minister and he made it a part of the funeral service.

You can't take it with you...or can you?

Buried in the Sky

Leonard was my favorite uncle, probably because he escaped the mold for Norwegian men. Instead of being tall, muscular, somber, and stoic like his brothers, he was small, animated, quick, and vociferous, and he had the quick sparkling eyes of his mother, Grandma Olson. Len was a photographer and a good one. He owned the Photo Arts Studio in LaCrosse, Wisconsin. When we were little kids, he would come to Minneapolis and Yellow Lake for a visit once or twice a year and photograph everything he could round up: kids, adults, dogs, toys, etc. He loved to do portraits and composite photos that told stories. Our best childhood photographs were taken by Uncle Leonard and he gave me my first camera, a Leica.

Len loved to take portraits and wedding photos for plain folks. He was an artist at getting people to relax and then clicking the shutter at just the beginning of a smile. Once he had the film developed, he was like a Rembrandt in his dark room. He could touch up a negative to remove skin blemishes and wrinkles, fill in balding heads, soften double chins and make other small improvements. The plain folks that he loved were always delighted when they received their photographs. Len did not like to photograph beautiful or rich people, especially women. They were never satisfied!

About the time Aldo Leopold was discovering his "shack" on the Wisconsin River, Len was setting up his "shack" on a trout brook in Pleasant Valley – one of the prettiest valleys in the southeastern Minnesota unglaciated landscape. He loved the Mississippi Valley and the limestone bluffs and picturesque hill farms. He and his wife Gladys had a garden, a trout pond, a German shepherd and a tame nuthatch named Charlie that would come when called and never missed a peanut thrown into the air. They also had a beagle named Snoopy with one of the sweetest "voices" I ever heard. When on a rabbit, it was music to hear his baying echoing off the hills and bluffs of Pleasant Valley.

Len and Glady provided the place for my weekend escapes when the pressure of college courses and five part-time jobs got too heavy. I would board the Hiawatha train on Friday and have a couple glasses of wine for the two-hour ride to LaCrosse. I arrived with "half a buzz" which was just the way we kept it for the whole weekend of photographing weddings, developing photos, catching fish, hunting rabbits with Snoopy, and discussing life and politics. Every couple hours we would pause for another glass of "Sneaky Pete," Len's favorite muscatel wine.

Rural weddings were the one thing I could really help Len with. Often when we arrived at the church, the wedding flowers and aisle runners were just left in a box on the front steps. We had to decorate the church and get the corsages and carnations on the members of the wedding party. While Len was busy photographing the basic wedding ceremony and reception, I was helping with the arrangements and lighting and getting to know the families. Then I would get the relatives together for group photographs. Often they had no other family pictures and Len would substantially increase his business with the extra family photos.

Len was quite a philosopher and his thoughts and words tended toward socialism, natural foods and living, equality for all, traditions of native people, suspicion of organized religion, and going to the "happy hunting ground" when he died. This all sounded pretty good to me, especially when diluted or reinforced with "Sneaky Pete." When Sunday evening came, I was thoroughly "relaxed." Len and Glady would help me onto the train and by the time I got back to the university, I was sober and ready to hit the books again.

When Len finally died after a period of failing health and Alzheimer's disease, his body was cremated and his ashes were scattered into the wind from one of the high limestone bluffs overlooking his beloved Pleasant Valley and the Mississippi River. Thus he was "buried in the sky" over his "happy hunting ground."

A Night with the Sioux

In the summer of 1960, I was in the third and final year of studying canvasback duck populations on the southern Manitoba prairies. After two previous summers of trying to use a camping tent or a travel trailer, each of which used half the daylight hours, I found that the most effective way to make the necessary observations of ducks at dawn and dusk was traveling alone with just my car, a sleeping bag, and some food and water in a cooler. I mostly just slept out on the ground or by a convenient haystack. Sometimes I tried to find a hot meal midday, or a motel room for a shower on rainy days.

One evening while driving to my next study area, I saw a line of 12 to 15 occupied military style tents on a hillside overlooking Oak Creek. This sudden presence of so much activity on the prairie got my attention and I drove over and found the annual gathering of part of the Sioux Indian nation. These were the descendants of the Sioux that crossed into Canada after the Battle of the Little Bighorn.

When I introduced myself and explained why I was there, I was warmly welcomed to stay and share their food and participate in the gathering. I shared a campfire with a group of tribal elders. In addition to several small family campfires, there were two large dance circles with bonfires and drummers in each. One circle was for the elders and adults and the other for children and young adults. In the adult circle, they danced alone to the beat of the drum while singing and praying. The men danced separately counterclockwise in the outer edge and the females danced singly on the inside in the opposite direction. In the youth circle, there was a variety of dances, including square dancing. Occasionally youths went to the adult circle to dance in the traditional way.

The elders I was sitting with were probably all grandparents. The grandmothers especially were as interested in me as I was in them. The way I was traveling and working and sleeping on the prairie alone was hard for them to understand and they wanted to know why I did so and if I was okay. In the Indian cultures aloneness (i.e. banishment) was a form of punishment for criminals and misfits. In their culture nobody could survive alone on the prairies.

These elders (who may have been children at the Battle of the Little Bighorn) explained to me how they came to be Canadians. After Custer was killed in the battle, the various tribes and Indian nations who participated dispersed widely to escape the retaliation of the U.S. Army that was sure to follow. These "Manitoba Sioux" crossed the Canadian border to where they received necessary local support and protection for a few years.

The elders told me their version of the Battle of the

Little Bighorn. General Custer was systematically attacking unprotected Indian villages and killing all of the adults and children. His tactic was to create a scenario away from each village to draw off the warriors on horseback and then go in and kill everyone else. The northern prairie Indians knew that they would be wiped out if Custer (Yellow Hair) was not stopped.

Warriors from several Indian nations gathered and hid around the Little Bighorn but left the village "open and vulnerable." A group of mounted warriors confronted Major Reno's cavalry unit and led them off in a chase several miles to the east. As Custer and his remaining soldiers began to attack the village, all of the hidden Indians came out, attacked and killed Yellow Hair. Then everyone had to disperse to try to avoid the wrath of the U.S. Army that followed.

After a long night of socializing, I slept on the ground by my truck parked at the end of the line of tents. Before dawn, I woke up and departed quietly to my next study area. The next time I drove by the hillside at Oak Creek, it was bare.

Searching for Grandfathers

As a small boy I had a severe handicap—no grandfathers! Both had died before I was born. No one to sit patiently and listen to my tall tales, no one to teach me how to whittle a stick to make a whistle, no one to advise me about proper behavior toward girls and women. To fill this void, I began to informally attach myself to grandfatherly types, a behavior that has lasted all my life.

Herman Battersby was a true "son of the prairies," one of the best no-book, self-taught naturalists I have ever known. He grew up on a rundown farm at Oak Lake, Manitoba and spent his whole life learning about the prairies. Because of his broad firsthand knowledge and excellent marksmanship, he was frequently recruited for scientific expeditions across the Canadian prairies.

Herman assisted me in my canvasback duck research project because Oak Lake and the broad surrounding marshes were part of my study area and he knew the access points and waterfowl movement patterns very well. Beyond his help in my busy scheduled research activities, he encouraged me to have lots of free time to really get to know and understand the prairies. Some of my most important research findings came on those days.

One day while just driving around looking for prairie chickens, we came upon a large slough with about 200 canvasback ducks on it. As was my habit, I immediately began recording sex and age ratios. Then about half the birds began flying around. Disgusted, I recorded the birds still on the water and found that the adult males had stayed while the adult females and juveniles had been flying around. This was the first inkling I had about differences in activity patterns—a big factor in hunting mortality.

There are lots of great memories of days afield with Herman Battersby.

One day Herman had caught a bunch of cutworm moths from under a rug hanging on the side of a shed. He was releasing them one by one for the Western kingbirds that were perched around his yard waiting. They never missed!

My best memory of Herman was the day he showed me an ancient buffalo skeleton exposed by the receding summer water levels of Oak Lake and I found the arrowhead that had killed the buffalo.

—

Robert Gaylord was the tenth and probably the most influential "grandfather" I found. Rather, he found me. A wealthy industrialist and sportsman from Illinois, he supported research on the breeding biology and population dynamics of canvasback ducks, my job for four years.

A number of wildlife agencies including the Delta Waterfowl

Research Station, Ducks Unlimited, the Canadian and United States Wildlife Services and several state and provinces were expecting and planning that my research would produce positive information with which to be optimistic about the status of canvasback duck populations. Instead, my research results did just the opposite. The methods, patterns and timing of hunting seasons and the draining of prairie wetlands reduced canvasback populations and reproductive potential by at least fifty percent and with the present canvasback hunting seasons and habitat loss, it is likely to continue indefinitely.

Bob Gaylord grew up and worked as a rancher in the western United States. He had western-personality characteristics. He patiently observed, had a good judgment of human character, was soft and sparsely spoken, and was careful in delicate situations.

He invited representatives of all the concerned agencies and me to his summer camp on a wilderness lake in north central Manitoba for a friendly get-together, a discussion about canvasbacks in government agencies' policies and propaganda (i.e. always more) and my research results. Naturally, these bureaucrats were doing everything they could to continue their present policies and optimistic propaganda. They were criticizing, minimizing or ignoring my research results. Bob Gaylord listened carefully to both sides but did not take a position.

One afternoon Bob and I were alone as he was cooking a large

4-inch thick Porterhouse steak on the coals from a wood fire. He was quietly thinking and all of a sudden said that he didn't know of any position anywhere in government or business where one could think like I did. He said that my independent thinking was a valuable ability, even with all the criticism. His words had a double meaning: 1) that he understood and respected my research and 2) that I would be an independent thinker the rest of my life.

Late that afternoon, an airplane landed at a newly constructed camp on the other side of Bob's wilderness lake and I was disappointed at the intrusion into the wilderness, especially with an airplane.

I said, "It's a shock. I wonder what this area will be 10 years from now."

Bob said, "Dave, if I'm here 10 years from now, I'll take it"—another thought for me to carry for the rest of my life.

I'll never forget Bob Gaylord dressed in his blue jeans, western boots, plaid shirt, and bandana around his neck, cooking a western style steak right on the coals and giving me some of the most important words I'd encounter for the rest of my life.

Small Places

A small town – three houses and a general store with board sidewalks and hitching rail, not much changed in a hundred years. Hidden in some minor mountains forty gravel miles off the interstate.

The Brer Rabbit Café in a southern town with a classic courtyard square. An old log cabin houses the historical society and a grandmotherly lady who defends the Confederacy in one corner and reads children stories by its famous author in another.

The Hummingbird Café where you can have breakfast with up to nine species of hummingbirds using the feeders on the veranda. So close to the crowded national parks and monuments that most people pass right by.

A crossroads community in Montana that celebrates the victory of Chief Joseph with a street dance on the intersection. The western beauty who tends bar at the Longhorn Saloon can turn a young man into a would-be cowboy even before he has a drink.

A New England town with a classic white church set in a green meadow by a crystal clear lake. The general store, post office and snack bar, housed in a single building, are all run by a lady who is also the chief of the volunteer fire department.

A mountain stream in Charlie Russell country. Its waters reflect all the colors in his famous paintings. Thankfully, this small remote stream has escaped the hordes of guides, drift boats and sports that now crowd the more famous trout waters.

These are a few of the dozens of beautiful small places that I have found in a lifetime of doing something else. Fact is, the best way to find beautiful small places is to keep your eyes open and just stumble into them. Some say that I should assemble all my small places together in a book and publish it so that others can enjoy them. But I won't; too many of my small places already exist only as memories of a certain time past.

In the 1950s, Jackson Hole, Wyoming was a beautiful small place with board sidewalks, hitching rails and real ranchers. At the end of summer they gathered together in town for a weekend of socializing before heading up into the high country to bring their cattle down for the winter. Now Jackson Hole is a Mecca for hordes of tourists who watch a fake stagecoach robbery every afternoon at three o'clock and then buy souvenirs made in China.

Brooksville is a collection of hamlets (North, West, Center, etc.) close by the ocean in down east Maine. In the 1950s, the residents fished and worked in the woods, granite quarries, and sawmills. They dug clams, raised blueberries, and sailed windjammers. If you listened carefully and spoke sparsely, you could enjoy the down east accents. In fall the deep blue water in protected harbors reflected lobster boats, schooners, dark green conifer forests, and the mahogany color of frosted blueberry fields. Now the harbors are filled with marinas, yachts, and diesel fumes; the scenic hillsides and blueberry fields are sprouting new mcmansions and the unique down east accent is a subject of ridicule in bars and nightclubs.

Beautiful small places help a person scratch down through the high-pressure-everything-for-sale clamor in our daily lives to discover what is really important. I hope you have some small places of your own and that you stumble on some more, but please don't advertise them.

The Need to Excel

Being the youngest son behind two older brothers and a sister is a tough life. Little brother Lloyd lived with hand-me-down clothes and half-broken toys and incomplete truths. He had to wait and watch as his older brothers and sister got to do things and go places that provided excitement and fun. It was always, "Stay with Mother," "There isn't room," "You're too young," "You don't know how," and "Scram."

Lloyd's life became even tougher after Mother's death when he was 14. Then her consoling wisdom was also absent. But as he waited and watched, the need to get into the act, to be part of the crowd and to excel was building and when his time finally came, excel he did—in all his endeavors, good and bad!

Before he could drive he hitchhiked with his friend Jim Leaf and they made some pretty extensive trips. They went to Canada just to look around and got across the border and back with a pack of lies about "visiting grandmother." His longest venture with the thumb was a tour of the west. When they ended up in a small Montana town broke and trying to sell a wrist watch for food, Dad got a call from the friendly sheriff telling him he could have his son back if he would send bus fare.

Lloyd found something he could really excel in on the high school gymnastics team. He was tremendously coordinated, he had Dad's fine sense of rhythm and he was fearless. He gave Henry High School and Coach Vally their first state championship. Some other aspects of high school such as grades and attendance were not so good; in fact, he knew Dean Barnes quite well from the frequent times I had to accompany him back to the Dean's office to get readmitted. (Incidentally, Dean Barnes and I were well acquainted from my high school escapades, but that's another story.) On the last trip to get Lloyd readmitted, shortly before graduation, Dean Barnes told me, "If I send him home one more time—don't bring him back."

Lloyd's graduation from high school was a joyous occasion—the last of four motherless kids had made it! But it was also brutal. In those days graduates marched across the stage and received their diplomas in order of their class standing. Lloyd was third from the last in over a hundred students. When Lloyd finally marched across the stage, I heard Dad mutter, "Whew. Thank God. I thought they were going to run out of diplomas before they got to Lloyd."

His driver's license gave Lloyd another arena in which to excel and he drove well, even better than Dad. He worked as a "runner" in the garage where Dad worked and was a favorite of the customers and Mr. Gillfilan (one of the owners), who always requested Lloyd as a driver when he had to get someplace in a hurry, even to Kansas City! Runners were the ones who drove customers to their offices or delivered cars or retrieved their cars from the parking area on the roof. One of his favorite stunts, performed with two other runners, was retrieving three cars at once. Three cars would come silently down the long curving ramp from the roof, bumper to bumper with the engines off and glide to a stop in front of the astonished customers. Each runner would exit with a flourish, wipe off the steering wheel and hold the door for the smiling customer. Jack Dean, the foreman, would mutter under his breath, "Goddam kids."

One Monday Dad got a call from the police in Forest Lake informing him that Lloyd (and Dad) were to appear in court to face speeding charges from a weekend arrest when Lloyd was returning from the cabin with a bunch of friends. After the fine was paid (the officer had reduced the speeding charge from 90 to 70 miles per hour) he complimented Dad on what an excellent driver Lloyd was. He knew he wasn't trying to avoid arrest, but it took him 21 miles to catch Lloyd and then only when he stopped at a railroad crossing.

While the rest of the family made do with good sensible used Fords, Lloyd had graduated to a Triumph roadster which became a kind of chariot to adventure. He gave me some rather exciting rides in it and indubitably there are some adventures that I don't even want to know about. The one that stands out in my memory is Lloyd's attempt to poach a deer, at night, with a bow and arrow, from the Triumph convertible. Lloyd's friend Ralph Malmberg was driving and Lloyd was sitting on top of the seat back. A nice buck jumped out onto the road in front of them and started running down the road. Lloyd said, "Step on it, Ralphy – I'll take him Indian style." Ralphy did as told and as the car shot ahead, Lloyd went out of the car backwards landing on his head in the road. As he was trying to shake the stars out of his head and check for broken bones and equipment, Ralphy had pulled up alongside the deer and was yelling, "Shoot him, Lloyd, shoot him!"

Lloyd's athletic ability led him to scholarships and a degree in athletic coaching at the University of Minnesota, where he was an outstanding gymnast. His fearless performances on the flying rings (nationally recognized) were the most beautiful I have ever seen. Performances on the flying rings have since been discontinued because of the severity of injuries to the performers.

After coaching at Marshall High School, Lloyd earned a Master's degree in coaching sports for handicapped children, created a program in the Minnesota schools, and became a national leader in that new field.

Not bad for my "left behind" little brother!

The Orange Indian

A used 1950s hippie van, christened the Orange Indian, was the chariot that carried me through my mid-life crisis.

My teaching at the university was getting stale, my marriage was falling apart, and I needed field observations of aspen tree regeneration and distribution to complete my research project. It was time for my third and final sabbatical. Since my travel plans would take me to many remote locations, I needed a vehicle that I could camp out in.

I asked my friend Smitty at the local garage to see if he could find me a used truck van that I could equip to camp out in. Soon he called back to say that he had found one but cautioned that it might "change my image." Wow—did it ever! Bright orange in color, it had mounted Indians painted on its sides, velour upholstery with tassels, mood lighting, stereo sound system, cherry bomb exhaust pipes, a truck sized air horn, and a two-person cozy bed across the back. I installed a rocking chair and portable desk and cooking equipment and I was good to go! It was perfect. I drove it for more than 170,000 miles, and took my two Brittany Spaniels, Iner and Katy, with me.

In the Durham community and around campus many people turned away in disgust when I blasted the air horn and let the cherry bomb pipes rumble but a lot of guys, including men of mid-life crisis age, gave me a raised fist salute. It was fun to show it to my students. The guys thought it was great but some of the coeds thought I was a dirty old man when they saw the cozy two-person bed and the tassels, mood lights, and stereo music.

The route of travel took me across southern Canada from Ontario to Saskatchewan and up and down mountains in the western states. I stopped to visit many old friends in Canada and the Midwest. My route and my sabbatical were planned with "malice aforethought." The van was noticed and admired by many people but made the most impressions on waitresses at wayside coffee shops—many a longing stare when I asked them if they wanted a ride in it.

With the addition of a pop-up sleeper tent on the roof, it had room for three people and I took my friend Socrates and brother Lloyd deer hunting and fishing in some of the best western trout streams.

After the six month sabbatical trip, I made several trips to Wisconsin and even used it in starting my Christmas tree plantation at home.

After about 170,000 miles, my time with the Orange Indian came to an end in western Ontario because of a broken cam shaft. In exchange for the cost of towing, the garage owner took possession of the Indian and I slept in it one last night while my friend Joe Vaillancourt went to rent a replacement. The garage owner's teenage son was already eyeing it and hoping it would be his chariot to adventure.

The Ouija Board

The late October weather had turned cool and a group of friends was gathered at our house in Durham to enjoy a fire on the hearth, the first of the season. The group included musicians Rick and Ron Shaw, Tommy Makem and their friends. The wine and snacks and conversations were flowing freely.

Ingrid Gsottschneider arrived late (again) and was even more agitated than usual. She was carrying her Ouija board, which she insisted was evil and had to be destroyed by burning. To avoid distractions, I offered to take it out to the farm and burn it in a brush pile later. However, she was insistent that it had to be destroyed now and placed it in the fireplace upright over the very hot coals. Almost immediately, the Ouija board, impregnated with many layers of flammable lacquers, was a sheet of flames which were shooting up into the chimney.

The chimney, with its 20 year accumulation of resinous sap from too many small, friendly fires, caught and we had a roaring, vibrating fire which shook the whole house. I told Ingrid it was the Devil coming out of her Ouija board and she was screaming, crying and hiding her face. Our wide-eyed guests abandoned their wine glasses and backed away from the fireplace. Jan quickly got a box of baking soda and used it to somewhat smother the flames. I followed with a bucket of water, but this did little to slow down the roaring fire up in the chimney. Jan called the Fire Department and I rushed outside to check the roof and the house. Like a huge blow torch, four feet of blue flames were shooting up out of our chimney!

By the time the firefighters arrived, the fire had somewhat burned itself out. The entire neighborhood was lit up with floodlights, flashing red lights and fire trucks. One firefighter took a huge logging chain up on the roof. He lowered it down into the chimney and shook and rattled it back and forth to dislodge burning embers and soot. Others had placed a huge tarp over the carpet to catch the debris.

After the firemen had made sure that the fire was out and the house was safe, they packed up their gear and departed. As they left, the chief asked me again what I had burned. I told him it was a Ouija board. He shook his head in disbelief and muttered,

"That's what I thought you said."

The Sunset

In the summer of 1988, I attended the National Christmas Tree Growers Convention in Bangor, Maine. I was searching for knowledge to help me in growing and managing trees on my small farm in Madbury, New Hampshire, but I soon became disillusioned by the gross commercialization of everything at the conference. I decided to retrace some of my travels of 30 years before and try to renew old memories.

I drove through the University of Maine campus at Orono and then up to 21 Veazy Street in Old Town. There were wonderful memories of Arthur and Eva Goldsmith who provided a warm comfortable apartment for us while I attended the university. Downtown the Goldsmith clothing store was still in business, operated by one of Grammy and Grandpa Goldsmith's sons. On the way back through Bangor, I passed the Eastern Maine General Hospital where Laurie (our "Mainiac") was born and the Salmon Pool where I used to watch bald eagles stealing fish from American mergansers.

After a stop to visit with my old professor Mal Coulter and his wife in Eddington, I headed down through Bucksport to the Brooksvilles and Blue Hill. My old hunting and fishing buddies

Crosby Ladd and John Howard were long since dead, but it was good to see the Howard, Ladd, Perkins, Congdon and other down east family names on the mailboxes. The Brooksvilles (North, South, Middle & East) and Blue Hill were still scenic and beautiful, but the million dollar "summer" houses sprouting up on the scenic hillsides and blueberry fields were disturbing, as were the "smoke pots" – diesel-powered pleasure yachts – now at anchor amongst the fishing boats and sailing schooners. Change is inevitable, but I tried to focus on my first impressions of this beautiful area. I'm finding it more and more difficult to return to beautiful places I have known in the past.

    I headed up the coast to Acadia National Park to watch the sunset on Cadillac Mountain. The top of Cadillac Mountain is famous for being the first place the rising sun hits in the United States, but I believe the sunset over America is much more important to contemplate. I was struck by the amount of bumper-to-bumper traffic in comparison to 30 years previously when you could drive completely around the Park, park anywhere along the road and scarcely see another vehicle. I passed the rocky ledge where Jan and I with Laurie (in diapers) picnicked and caught pollack from the ocean. The road up Cadillac Mountain was jammed and there was no parking available within a quarter mile of the top. Whereas I used to come here alone, the top of the mountain was now crowded with "yuppies," hundreds of them with wine flasks, waffle-stomper boots, short leather pants and bandanas or backwards caps on their heads. I felt out of place with my camouflage hunting cap and worn chamois shirt.

There was talk and radios and drinking all over the mountain, but as the sun began to set, it became quieter and quieter and then all quiet – you could have heard a pin drop. Just as the sun sank below the horizon, there was spontaneous applause from everywhere! They know! They understand! And they respected one of the great mysteries of life and the driving force of our existence.

I left the mountain with a feeling of peace and tranquility and faith that things on earth will work out alright in the long run.

Jenny Wren

One of my favorite memories is Grandma Peterson in her easy chair under the large bushy burr oak tree by the gate to the barnyard. Tena was a strong-willed woman who lived and farmed alone for many years. After finishing her morning chores, Tena would come shuffling back from the barn and sink into her easy chair with a sigh of relief to listen to her "Jenny Wren" sing from the lower branch which had a nest box.

In contrast to the barnyard, the house yard was immaculate and well-tended, with flower beds and planters, carefully pruned evergreens and white painted fence – it was her summer refuge! After she had relaxed a bit, she would take off her four-buckle overshoes (barn shoes) and her sheepskin moccasins which she wore to work in. Her feet, ankles and legs were so twisted and arthritic that no other shoes or boots fit. Then "Topsy" her pet terrier would lick her toes and feet while Grandma sighed in relief and proclaimed Topsy as the best medicine for her aching feet. Tena believed in Christian Science healing and did her best to avoid doctors of any kind.

Grandma believed that her "Jenny Wren" came and sang just for her when she sat in her chair and that "she" was the sweetest bird alive. As I was studying ornithology at the university, I learned the true breeding behavior of house wrens and that her "Jenny" was really an entrepreneurial "Billy" who had built nests in every nook, cranny and nest box in the yard and was busy singing by each one to attract as many females to him as possible. The female wrens, on the other hand, were onto his philandering ways and would sneak into the nests of other females and peck holes in their eggs.

One day after I had been fishing and brought some trout, we were listening to "Jenny" sing. I told Tena about the breeding behavior of her wrens. Tena would have no part of it. She let out a loud Norwegian "Uff Da" and that was the end of that! Now we have house wrens in our yard and I too would rather believe the humanized version of their lives.

A Young Dog

A cold raw drizzly April morning is just not suitable for outdoor work on the Christmas trees. After Marsha leaves for work, I treat myself to a few chapters of *Blue Highways* and then a nap on the couch in front of the fireplace. Patches, our nine-month-old English Setter, having watched Marsha's truck disappear down the driveway, joins me on the couch tucked in behind my legs. We share the couch, the warmth, and the nap.

After about an hour there is a long English Setter nose snuffling in my face, communicating to me that it's time to take a walk and check out the local bird populations. She dutifully rings the bell hanging from the door knob and softly mouths my hand to tell me there is some urgency in her need to go. Who says that dogs cannot talk? While I pull on my rain gear and boots, Patches waits with her nose at the crack in the door. When I open the door, she is out like a flash but only takes two steps and freezes into an expectant point. With her, it's always first things first as her head slowly swings, her eyes looking for birds or squirrels and her nose testing the breeze.

As we walk through the chilly damp woods, I'm a little resentful that my warm nap was abbreviated but also appreciative of a young dog that keeps me from turning into a 73-year-old couch potato. Patches knows my land better than I do and her walk consists of a series of slow stealthy sneaks from one birdy location to the next with occasional points when the scent is fresh. Not until she has checked a couple hundred yards of her territory (my woods) does she stop to relieve herself – first things first!

There are places in the Christmas tree plantation that Patches considers as her exclusive territory and despite my commands, she bolts ahead to freeze on point and then rush excitedly through the trees, flushing all the juncos and field sparrows that have paused migration to feed on the seeds of annual grasses and hide from the weather by roosting in the artificially thick foliage of cultured Christmas trees. I feel guilty about the messy unkempt appearance of my plantation, but to Patches this is the best – full of birds and scent and with birds to flush behind every tree. Perhaps the trade-off is a good one. Despite the focused narrowmindedness of humans, Mother Nature is constantly trying to make the land useful to all in her care.

On mild sunny afternoons Patches sits on the porch or by the garden and watches for birds, squirrels or chipmunks in the paddock where Deacon and Ditty are grazing. When she sees some crows alight to pick the waste oats out of horse manure, she takes off at a dead run to chase them away. In the process, she frequently gets Deacon and Ditty running and kicking up their heels. When they have settled down, Patches will often approach Deacon and lick his face and muzzle and Deacon will in turn nuzzle or chew Patches' hair and collar. Maybe a young dog is good for old horses as well as old men?

Patches hasn't caught a bird yet but she has caught many mammals including mice, voles, moles, chipmunks, and a muskrat. When she catches one, she often plays with it cat-like for hours, throwing it into the air, shaking it, pawing it and running with it in her mouth. She brings each of her catches to show us, but wants to tease us into chasing her. It's really comical to see her expression with just a long tail of a mouse hanging out of her mouth. Most impressive for us was the large muskrat she caught in the beaver pond. I've seen several dogs horribly cut up by muskrats but Patches didn't have a scratch on her. She had a great time showing her muskrat off to Marsha and me (for several days!) but couldn't understand why Deacon Black wasn't impressed with her prize.

As each afternoon draws to a close, Patches becomes more and more attentive toward watching the driveway and waiting for Marsha's truck to come up the road. Sometimes she will wake up out of a nap and jump up on the couch and stare down the road just two or three minutes before Marsha arrives. She must be able to sense that Marsha is near and has stopped at the mailbox. Like me, she shares the joy of Marsha's arrival but she is much better at anticipating the exact moment. Now she is all attentive and it's first things first again. This young dog's joyful welcome is the beginning of the best part of Marsha's day and it makes my day complete and wonderful.

Charlie Church's Barn

Charlie's horse barn is a hole in the ground surrounded by a circle of piled soil and horse manure and covered by aspen trees cut in early fall to hold their leaves all winter long. When the 30-foot-wide hole was dug, the soil was removed down to below the frost zone so that the constant 53° temperature of the earth partially warms the barn. The accumulation of decaying horse manure also supplies some heat. The aspen tree cover provides shade in summer and protection from wind and snow and some reduction in body heat loss by radiation to the sky. The horses enter and leave by going over the circle of soil and through gaps in the aspen trees. This "barn" is used year round, providing warm protection in winter and a cool shady fly-free refuge in summer.

I saw this barn in North Central Manitoba being used by two big blond Belgian draft horses in the summer of 1960 and recently I have found what I believe to be a similar but larger "hole in the ground" barn used by the first settlers in Madbury, New Hampshire.

Charlie Russell's Palette

In my view, Charlie Russell is still the premiere painter of the West. He had a way of portraying the scope and rhythms of the Western landscapes while still including some of the messiness that is always there. His cowboys and Indians and horses all reflect their hard lives in being thin, rawboned, worn and edgy, and each of his paintings tells a story better than words. The colors in his paintings truly tell of dry, dusty landscapes with the many yellows, browns and grays, yet there are also shades of purple, mauve, orange and red which add excitement and beauty to his paintings. In my wanderings around all the states in the West, I've looked for these interesting colors and not been able to see them.

On my last trip I visited the Russell Museum in Great Falls, Montana and was somewhat turned off by the newly painted buildings, fresh green manicured lawns and neat offices. There was only one room with some of Russell's things, but the whole setup just didn't feel like Charlie Russell's West. I carefully checked as many original paintings and early prints as possible to see if these interesting shades of purple, blue, mauve, orange and red were there. They were; they had not been added afterward and they were not artifacts of printing presses. When I left, I was still enthralled with Charlie Russell's paintings, but more confused than ever.

We headed south over the Big Belt Mountains for a stay at my favorite campsite among the teepee rings on the Smith River. After some wonderful trout fishing, we headed northeast over the Little Belt Mountains toward the Judith Basin, a place that I had heard and read much about but never seen. As we descended the south branch of the Judith River, we came upon the Charlie Russell memorial wayside. Since it was getting late, we decided to camp for the night. We cooked in the fireplace and ate on the picnic table. At sunrise, I discovered all the colors that Charlie Russell had ever used in his paintings. We were surrounded by rock ledges and cliffs that included all the purples, blues, mauve, oranges and reds of the Russell paintings and the rising sun showed them off in all their glory. We also explored the middle branch of the Judith and found we could walk right up to boulders and ledges and touch and feel the colors. This was truly Charlie Russell country and we were touching his palette.

One in Ten Thousand?

Completely golden sunrises are spectacularly beautiful occurrences but extremely rare. Fortunately, I have experienced three in my lifetime and I constantly hope and look for another.

Once on the ocean I was watching for the "emerald flash" of color that appears on the horizon just above and before the sun breaks the horizon. Instead, everything was suddenly bathed in golden light. The ocean appeared to be liquid gold and our boat, bodies, faces, hair all turned to gold. There were no shadows, only the warm, peaceful golden light for about ten minutes. The beautiful peaceful feeling in our bodies lasted for a while longer.

Once again at dawn I was driving up the west side of Lake Winnipesaukee to meet Rebecca for breakfast on a cloudy overcast morning when suddenly everything turned to gold. I parked in a scenic overlook and viewed a completely golden lake, landscape, sky, me, my car and the highway. I stood still, entranced in a mood of peaceful serenity that lasted about fifteen minutes until the grey light and shadows of a cloudy day returned.

On the train headed west to California I loved to watch the Rocky Mountains seemingly rise up out of the prairies as we travelled. One cloudy morning at dawn the prairies and mountains were suddenly bathed in golden light but the normal light still existed on the train. It was like viewing a beautiful painting or movie out of the window. I now understood why there were tales of "mountains of gold" in the minds of early explorers and prospectors.

Completely gold sunrises occur only when there is a complete low hanging cloud layer except for a narrow band of sky where the sun rises in the east. All the light rays of the rising sun are trapped below this cloud layer and reflected back and forth in all directions, bathing everything in gold light without shadows. As soon as the rising sun is obscured by clouds, it all disappears.

It's possible to experience some of the peace and serenity of golden light with tinted light bulbs or in front of a fireplace or by an outdoor campfire, but nothing compares with a golden sunrise.

The Changeover

Of the four seasons, summer is the hardest to let go. Fall is easy – one day it snows and then it's winter. Winter is also easy, but spring is often slow in coming. Spring simply slides into summer without a transition, but admitting to the end of summer is hard.

At Lloyd's cabin on Wood Lake the day after Labor Day, I'm reluctant to let summer go and I need a couple days for the transition. Lloyd, Socrates and I are just back from three weeks of trout fishing and camping out in the Rockies. We fished 23 trout streams and lakes in 16 days – what a trip! Now I have to think about a return to bureaucracy, schedules and classes – but first some time for me!

I spend a day puttering around with minor repairs to the dock, new tie-downs for the pontoon boat and picking up around the yard. Wood Lake is wonderfully quiet and peaceful after the summer speed boats and crowds have gone and school has started. I do some reading and have a nap in the sun. After dark I take a naked swim – just me, the dark still warm water and the moon and stars.

The next day I wash clothes at the Laundrymat in Grantsburg – the only place I know where you can wash clothes and watch the geese flying down Main Street on their way to Memory Lake to rest and digest their morning feed of waste corn and grass plucked from nearby farms. After lunch at the Hallway Café, I drive around town recalling the events and places from my childhood summers. At Pine Hill Cemetery I water the flowers and pay my respects to the graves of Dad and Mother, my grandparents and many aunts, uncles and cousins. In the evening I drive around the Crex Meadows Wildlife Area. The white-tailed deer fawns are still spotted and half grown, and the Sandhill crane chicks are well developed and rusty red. I even see a bald eagle and wonder if it's the one that Dad claimed as his – they are long-lived.

I watch the sunset over the marshy ponds I call "my reflecting pools." This is my favorite place to watch sunsets because there are few trees and I get a real sense of the prairies in the vast expanse of sky reflected in the water. This evening there is a single towering thunderhead reflected in the pools along with a family of trumpeter swans. I return to camp feeling a little guilty about the friends, family and responsibilities waiting in New Hampshire.

In the morning I sleep late, have a leisurely shower, clean up the cabin and pack the truck. No need to leave early and drive into the rising sun; it's less than a full day's drive to a sleep over at Sault Ste. Marie, Michigan. Public radio accompanies me across the beautiful wild northern Wisconsin landscape. The last stop in Wisconsin, the land of my birth, is the friendly welcome center at Hurley.

Once in Michigan I need the music of Willy Nelson and Merle Haggard to keep heading east. Now my objective is lunch at the Do Drop Inn, a rundown roadside restaurant in the wilds of the Upper Peninsula. I only stop here a couple times a year but the cook/waitress remembers me. I feel welcome, and she often has excellent Lake Superior whitefish on the menu. More assistance from Willie and Merle and I can gas up at Marquette. I pass the motel in Munising where someone tried to steal a deer we had tied on the trunk of Mark's Mustang. Iner stopped the theft by barking in the middle of the night. Now there is time for a nap on the shore of Lake Superior with the sound of the waves to put me to sleep. The final push to Sault Ste. Marie includes 25 miles of absolutely flat straight Highway 17 and many places I used to stop when Katy or Iner had to pee.

The last day of driving is a long one. I leave the motel before dawn and drive as far as possible before sunrise. I pass the truck stop where I used to sleep over in my truck when I didn't have money for a room. If the sunrise is cloudless, I stop for breakfast and rest my eyes while the sun rises. Across Ontario and New York is a long hard drive – maybe I'll be home by midnight. The need to be back with family and friends is sharper now and I'm thinking about classes to teach this fall. Then I remember Marsha – the pretty lady in my spring classes. She is signed up for my fall class. I press the accelerator a little harder. The summer is over!

The Boost

After graduating from high school, I bounced around for a couple years including: working in a Ford garage, a summer trying to become a woodsy hermit in northern Wisconsin, leading YMCA canoe campers in the Boundary Waters, a few weeks at a community college in Kansas City, an attempt to enroll in the submarine corps, and boxing in the Golden Gloves (I still have a broken nose).

Finally I began working in a greenhouse learning to grow all kinds of flowers. It was good, interesting year-round work — indoors and warm in the winter and in and out in the summer. I fit right into the groove of a steady unionized job. I was satisfied, fat, happy, and dumb!

One day my employer, Richard Rosacker, came by and told me my job was a "dead end" and I would end up doing the same thing for forty years. He told me I should quit, look around and check out some courses at the nearby University of Minnesota. To accommodate my financial needs, he made arrangements for me to work part-time at nights and on weekends and holidays. I did as he suggested and found all kinds of interesting courses and possibilities which eventually led to several degrees and service in the Air Force.

Getting out of the rut of steady full-time employment was not without hazards and jealousy. One of my co-workers reported me to the Teamsters Union. One night while I was working alone, two big union "goons" appeared out of the dark and asked me what the hell I was doing. We had a discussion and I told them if they forced me not to work here, I would tell my boss and the newspaper and that publicity would not be good for the Teamsters Union. They left.

Another problem came from Arlene, my high school girlfriend, who thought that the full-time steady job was the ticket to marriage. She was ready and the pressure on me became intense. One day she abruptly left to visit her older married sister in Portland, Oregon and ten days later she was married!

At the university I was able to enroll as an "adult special." In that category, I could take any course or courses I wanted. Naturally I chose the most interesting courses in several different programs. I sort of shopped around: horticulture, wildlife, bee keeping, and geology. In order to graduate with a Bachelor's degree, I had to register full-time for one year and fill in the prerequisites like mathematics, statistics, botany and zoology. I managed to complete the normal four year program in wildlife management in five and a half years.

I am really happy that one day while traveling in Florida, I was able to look up Richard Rosacker and thank him for the "boost" that got me going towards a more interesting life.

The Life of my Canoe

It's mid-February and my canoe, overturned on a stack of lumber and partially covered with snow, is in a mid-winter sleep. Recalling many days on dancing waters and plans for future trips, I realize my canoe, like the mystical village at Brigadoon, lives only when I choose to give it life.

It speaks with creaks and rattles when I pick it up and whispers with a long slow swish when I launch it in the welcoming water. There it rides, alive and bouncy, responding to each little wavelet and breeze. It is so alive and ready to go that I have to hold it steady lest it slip away on a trip of its own. With even pressure on my butt and knees, it tells me the load is centered and the balance is just right for easy travel. With the first light stroke of the paddle, my canoe turns, seeking the right direction. With the next harder stroke of the paddle, the bow surges up and blows bubbles along the sides, an expression of satisfaction for being on the move again. By slipping off course to port or starboard, my canoe tells me how frequently I have to J or sweep to keep the selected heading.

Somehow my canoe senses my moods and plans, adjusting accordingly, whether slow steady progress when trolling a fly or the quiet glide when viewing the sunset or the reflections of cardinal flowers and pickerel weed along the shadowed shorelines. It also assists when there is a fish on the line. If the fish is on the starboard line, it turns slowly to starboard so that the fish comes alongside for netting. My canoe is impatient and doesn't care much for still fishing, eventually swinging or pulling on the anchor line or slipping away from the chosen waters. It seems to appreciate a change in scenery as much as I do.

Once my friend Colin felt that my canoe needed less paddling and more power. He brought over a bracket and attached an electric motor. My canoe didn't appreciate it and, like a newly harnessed colt, caused all kinds of problems – running too fast, hitting rocks and tangling up weeds and fishing lines. It was like an overdose of steroids. When the motor was removed, our pleasant partnership resumed and I promised never to do that again.

When, after a day on the water and a glorious sunset, we turn toward home and begin some long, deep paddling strokes, the canoe surges ahead. With each stroke and the rhythm of our work my thoughts drift back to the many canoe lives I have shared and the many miles we traveled together.

In the 40s and 50s there were many canvas-covered cedar canoes that carried me hundreds of miles through the Boundary Waters of Minnesota and Ontario (my second job). These sturdy crafts were excellent for their tasks. They held a steady course in the wind, slid over rocks in the rapids and were easily repaired with balsam pitch, slices of tamarack, and spruce roots. These canoes tended to soak up water with days of continual use and became heavier to portage. The increased weight was somewhat offset by the decreased weight in the food packs. Also, it caused us to rest on portages and enjoy some of the magnificent scenery of the Quetico Superior.

In the 60s and 70s I shared the lives of many aluminum canoes that accompanied me in field research and teaching and occasionally took me on fishing expeditions. Although difficult in the wind, these canoes were sturdy, required less maintenance and could be used in salt water. So light, some without keels, they practically floated on the dew and were excellent in marshes. The big problem with aluminum canoes is their tendency to stick on rocks rather than slide over. It seems they almost have an attraction to rocks. My canoe and I have shared some of our lives together stuck on rocks!

There is one canoe that I really feel sorry for, a beautiful canoe made of birch bark and cedar whose life is seriously curtailed. It has only felt life on the water once when newly made, and since has been stored in the rafters of my friend Joe's garage. What a shame! Of course there are many canoes in this perpetual sleep; their owners never learned that they have to share their lives.

It seems that my canoe is most alive in the diminishing light of evening when we are traveling over smooth inky black water that reflects the sky and clouds like a mirror. It is said that lakes and waters are the eyes of the earth. If so, we are then floating in the pupil of the eye of the earth.

When it is time, my canoe finds the landing in the dark shadows of the shoreline and glides to a soft crunching stop on the sand. There are the usual creaks and rattles of protest as I place my canoe on its sleeping place. I hope that the paddles and fishing rods tucked inside provide some assurance that we will share our lives together again soon.

Poems

Diamonds

A cold clear February morning. I'm the richest man alive.
My fields of snow are sprinkled with diamonds,
Dead stalks in the garden transformed into fairy wands
Breezes in the pines fill the air with diamond dust
On snowshoes I walk on diamonds, apologetic for each step.

Many never see these diamonds–polarized lenses make them disappear
Soon plowed into dirty drifts, scraped, covered and salted
They are transformed before the sun is ready
How drab and dirty the urban winter landscapes
People there spend lives pursuing cruel, hard, sterile diamonds.

Come March the sun transforms my diamonds in many ways
Some stay to prepare the garden for lettuce, beans and gladiolus
Others rest in my well 'till called forth to water horses or make lemonade
Some ride the air to far away places, perhaps to slake a desert thirst
Others escape down the brook and river to taste the salt of the ocean
Some become mother's milk nursing new babies into the grand circle of life.

Come next February diamonds will return to sprinkle my fields of snow
Sparkling and shimmering in the sunlight–ready for new adventures.

Feeding Dinosaurs

Have you ever
fed a dinosaur?
Many people do
every day

On their porches
in back yards
or flower gardens
or on their lawns

I wonder if all
these people
believe in
evolution

Spring Thaw

First warm sunny morning

Snow melt dripping steadily

From newly exposed roofs

Horses with blankets off

Rolling in soft wet snow

Chickadees in all directions

Singing "Spring is here-here"

Red-winged blackbirds

Protecting a frozen marsh

Warm northwest breezes

More warm days ahead

Our long-awaited rewards

For months of cold and snow

Mother's Bleeding Heart

In our garden
We have a large
Beautiful
Bleeding heart
It helps me
Remember my mother
And childhood home
In the Depression years
Of the thirties
Urban landscapes were
Sparse and gritty
There was little money for lawns,
Shrubs, trees or flowers

Our yard in Minneapolis
Was typical or worse
No trees or shrubs
And only one flower
The coal trucks drove
Over our small lawn
To dump coal right
Into the basement

In the spring
Mother taught her
Brood of four
To watch a spot
In the narrow band
Of dirt between
The sidewalk and
The house foundation

One day as if
By magic small
Cinnamon colored buds
Were poking up
Through the coal dust

And debris
We were fascinated and
Mother was elated

Soon the buds were leafy shoots
That grew into
Long curved stems
With many small
Pink and white
Heart-shaped flowers
Like tiny bleeding hearts

Though her plant
Was small and constricted
Mother was happy
And enlisted our help
To protect her bleeding heart
Against dogs, cats, tricycles
Coal deliveries and footsteps
Never fertilized or watered
In its limited space the small bleeding heart
Survived all the years
We lived in the house

The exposure to
And devoted care
Of the bleeding heart
May have had a lasting effect
On us kids
My brother Don grew
Thousands of flowers

In his greenhouses
I grow thousands
Of Christmas trees on my farm
My brother Lloyd provides plants
For his church and cemetery
My sister Darielle tends
Her flower gardens in Philadelphia

Hard Memories

Thoughts of loved ones
are hardened in cemeteries
Names carved in granite
poor substitutes for
stories, dreams and photos

Memorial Day visits
flowers, flags on graves
parades and speeches
Memories and thoughts soon
left at cemetery gates

Our bodies are temporary
and belong to the earth
In grief we interrupt
Nature's marvelous process
of reclaiming our bones

Spirits of loved ones
alive in each of us
are maintained through love
and cannot be stored
on stone or in the ground

Logging at Bel Ami Farm

The saw bites, a tree falls
Shorn of its branches
Trunk unbroken and straight
Carefully skidded to landing
A trained eye and sharp saw
Make logs, pulpwood and fuel
To leave on waiting trucks

Rewards of forestry are many
Jobs, income, profits, taxes and lumber
A forest more open and inviting
For people, wildlife and flowers
More nutrients and sunlight
For saplings to flourish
The next forest is growing

In the new openings
Sunlight warms the soil
Seeds germinate and enter
The grand circle of life
A future forest is started
Mother Nature has provided
More gifts from the land

Senior Gravity

As we grow older
The force gets stronger
With passing time
The earth reminds us
Our bodies are borrowed

Shrinking by inches
We are closer
Lifts in shoes, tall hats
And hair piled higher
We practice illusion

Naps for seniors
Are daily reminders
Just try getting up
From a soft bed
Without extra effort

Overstuffed chairs
Divans without arms
Toilets too low
Where is the furniture
Designed for elders

More attention to feet
In less stylish shoes
With shorter steps
We watch the ground
And use a cane

Wheelchairs and automobiles
Are temporary reprieves
Even stretchers and gurneys
Finally give way to
Earth's welcoming presence

Family Photos

There they are
All stacked together
In a shoe box
Beside my desk
Photos from a hundred years
Passed down from
Generation to generation
Many without dates
Places or names

Old portraits—
Grandparents in high stiff collars
Engagements and weddings
New babies with mothers
Confirmations and bar mitzvahs
Graduations and military uniforms
Pets, toys and automobiles
Occasionally a funeral
Photographic Christmas cards

Seldom looking at them
I'm feeling guilty
They should be in albums
Or framed
Maybe I should sort
And discard
Yet when I see them
There are many memories

Some people believe
That the human spirit dies
Only when no longer remembered
Maybe my shoebox is stacked
With human spirits
I think I'll wait
And pass these family photos
Down to the next generation

Love Circles

More than round disks
of crunchy goodness
homemade cookies are
personalized, mobile, lasting
expressions of love

As a boy, no day's
adventures were complete
without Mother's
cookies in my pocket
to provide love and nourishment
even when reduced to crumbs

In later years
bags of these love circles
accompanying my long drives,
hunting and fishing trips
were rationed one per day
to extend the affection

My most lasting love circle
is a silver dollar
pressed into my palm
with tearful words
"remember me always"
by my Japanese lady

No Silken Pillow

When I die
No silken pillow
For my head
No fancy coffin
Or concrete vault

No floral arrangements
No preservatives
No perfumes or powder
No fancy new clothes
Or manicured nails

Nature reclaims bodies
In wonderful ways
But it's not pretty
Trying for beautiful
Makes it grotesque

Clothe my body in
Good old clothes with
My head on earth
In a shallow grave
Or recycle with fire

Carroll Varney, Guardian Angel

Raw-boned,
Unshaven,
Gravel-voiced,
Opinionated,
Driving an old pickup,
        he didn't look like an angel.

Patrolling the roads at night,
Announcing the presence of problems,
Monitoring the police radio,
Parked by our pasture at dawn,
Making sure we were up and moving,
        some called him a busybody.

Maintaining order at public accesses,
Assisting our conservation officers,
Picking up trash on roadways,
Helping families with troubles,
Providing firewood and contractor services,
        a productive senior citizen.

A raw chunk of humanity,
Rescued from lonely bachelorhood,
Molded into a loving husband,
A proud father and grandfather,
A distinguished veteran,
        improved by a loving wife.

Alert for problems in construction,
Intolerant of fools, fakes and blowhards,
Anticipating our needs with the right tools,
Ready to step in and help,
Prompt, professional and practical,
        a steady hand for novices.

Watching for tomatoes in gardens,
Happy when extras were planted for him,
He liked to pick them and call it "stealing,"
Often he "stole" them before I was awake,
Delighted when I added flowers to his "stolen" fruit,
        he loved stewed tomatoes.

Called forth to other guardian duties,
He didn't say he was departing,
His spirit guides my use of his tractor,
I check by the pasture –perhaps he is watching.
I plant extra tomatoes and hope they are "stolen,"

        We miss our Guardian Angel.

Holiday Beginning

On a snowy day
Take a saw
Pull a sled
Walk and search
For a special
Christmas tree
Thank Mother Nature
Cut and drag it in

Snuggle to the fire
Have a cookie
Sip hot cider
Meet old friends
See new babies
Watch kids grow
Exchange holiday wishes
Christmas has started

Junk Mail

Trees are cut
and changed to paper

Laced with chemicals
and fancy coatings

Delivered all over
and never read

Our postal system
paid by the ton

When I receive
seventeen duplicates

Of political ads
I'm convinced

This candidate can't
manage anything

A Grand Piano

There is a strange
Little building
In woods below
Rattlesnake Mountain
Containing only
A Grand Piano

A lonesome place
Distant from ears
Solitude, practice,
Teaching or mourning?
Perhaps a piano
That's been stolen?

While overlooking
The mountain heights
With bird songs
Whispering breezes
And distant
Calling of loons

Piano music
Drifted up from below
Blending beautifully
With wilderness sounds
A concert fit
For a mountain

Final Destination

A small brown leaf
Out of place
On March snow
Scurrying around
In gusty winds
Seeking a niche
For life's completion
In compost below

What a metaphor
For our lives

Born in loving sunlight
From a sturdy parent
Days dancing in breezes
Giving food and growth
To life's partners
Returning to earth
Our bodies needed
For new beginnings

Poinsettias

A patch of poinsettias
All clumped together
On the concrete floor
Ready for discard
On December 26

Still alive and beautiful
The various shades of
Red, yellow, orange and white
All mixed together
Like a painting
By a Dutch master
This bright display
Now unseen by most and
Ignored by all

Why
Do we allow a calendar
To determine our taste
For beauty and color
Even in the middle
Of winter?

My small prayer
Is that the vitality
Of these plants
Go into a compost pile
To flow again soon
Rather than be buried
For generations—deep
In a "sanitary" landfill

Second Floor Nurses

They have: Soft steps
                Comforting words
                Warm hands
                Smiling eyes

They are: Working mothers
                Mothers-to-be
                Students in training
                Devoted husbands

They help: Protect privacy
                Humor adversity
                Endure visitors
                Respect life (and death)

They are: Computer whizzes
                Masters of tubing
                Machine operators
                Chemical geniuses

Best of all–

  They have: Small needles

Circles of Stones

A perfect hilltop campsite
Breezy and a great view
A trout stream below
No firewood nearby but
Many ancient teepee rings

Well used by ancestors
Years of overlapping rings
Cooking stones and flint chips
Small ring in larger ring
A medicine man's abode

To honor this special place
We camped nearby
Enjoyed the historic view
Cooked with dry cow-flops but
Wished for real buffalo chips

Reluctant to leave
The memory kept for years
Returned to show a friend
Now a bulldozed parking lot
Another sacred place destroyed

Little Leaves

Like fancy decorations
They come in spring
All pastel shades of
Green yellow red gold

The bright open forest
Reveals branches birds and nests
A golden sunlight shines
On spring flowers below

Distant forest vistas are
Rounded mounds of pastel colors
Enjoy them while you can
Soon it's all shaded tunnels

Loss of Contact

One of the biggest failures of
modern education and medicine is
that the importance of human
contact with the earth
has been neglected or overlooked

All humans require daily
bare skin contact with earth's
electrical fields to
rebalance and maintain optimal
functions of our internal organs,
blood, skin and nervous system

This contact is called
Earthing or Grounding. It restores and
maintains the optimal balance
between negative and positive ions
in our bodies

As we have developed modern
dwellings and lifestyles
we have insulated ourselves
from the earth with shoes, beds,
chairs, floors, plastic, rubber, asphalt
and automobiles, trains and airplanes

Further, the increased use of
electrical equipment like stoves, radios,
television, microwaves and cell phones is
creating more harmful positive ions which
enter our bodies and disrupt normal
healthy functions

While the best earthing is through
the soles of our bare feet while
walking in wet grass or in sea water;
for people living, sleeping and working
indoors there are a variety of
devices to reconnect us to the earth

As these new earthing devices become
more widely known and used there will be
marked reductions or improvements in
many current health problems
especially in the more "developed"
societies of the earth

My Good Friend

Made my life interesting
Heard my stories
Understood my feelings
Gave good advice
Warned me of trouble

Encouraged me to try
Offered to help
Hunted with me
Fished with me
Cooked for me

Laughed with me
Aged with me
Shared good memories
Mourned with me
Died too soon

Happy Eternity!

The Wheelwright Jig
(Best Performed on Smooth, Slippery Ice)

Dragging their sleds
They go on the ice
Checking for landmarks
The spot is chosen
With circle two-steps
The holes are drilled
In setting the rods
The stage is set

Waiting and watching
Fish tales are told
Heads and bodies turning
Alert for the signal
To start the jig
A flag goes up
A rod tips down
The dance begins

Henry crosses the stage
In a high-stepping rush
Colin does the slip-slide
And lands on his back
Lee makes a diving grab
His arm down the hole
Dave loses a fish
The air turns blue

Pete stands and jigs
And catches a crappie
Richard pulls hard
And breaks his line
Craig sits and waits
On a hook without bait
Laurie shuffles and slips
And catches a perch

Fish flopping on ice
Increases the tempo
The action is fast
The sun is setting
Lines are tangled
The bait is gone
How many rods
Went down the hole

The dance ends at dark
Bags full of crappies
Whose is the biggest
He caught the most
With plans to return
And stories to tell
Dragging their sleds
They leave the ice

Addiction

Every day at sunrise
I'm drawn to the stove
For my morning fix
Coffee makes my day

My focus is sharper
Plans are developing
Priorities are established
Progress is possible

Limited to one cup
By an aging body
I sip and savor
and dream of tomorrows

Tall Ships

Out of Atlantic mists they come
Sails rising over the horizon
Majestic and silent they glide
Over waters cluttered with boats
Sails furled they rest in port
Open to land-bound visiting hordes

Quietly they leave on morning tides
Sails unfurling to catch the breezes
Slowly they turn on chosen courses
Golden sunlight setting sails aglow
Bearing our dreams and blessings
Into the Atlantic mists they go

Funerals

For a child
They are mysteries

For young adults
They are interruptions

For adults
They are tragedies

For seniors
They are memorials

For the elderly
They are homecomings

Indoor Wildlife

Our log house is an
Excellent habitat
For two species—
Dust bunnies and
Cob webbies

They propagate in corners
And inhabit
The many cracks in walls
And spawn under furniture
And behind pictures

They seldom use the carpets, rugs or
Linoleum floors where
The predatory vacuum cleaner
And broom are waiting

Sedentary most of the time
They are well behaved
But on sunny days or
When guests arrive
Out they come

Then the dust bunnies
Accumulate stray dog and cat hairs,
To become larger and mobile
And roll across the hardwood floors

Not to be outdone,
The cob webbies suddenly
Extend from the rafters
And come down to
Decorate the fieldstone
Fireplace and lamps

Skinning Mother Earth

After the glaciers receded
it took ten thousand years for
Mother Earth to make a productive
top soil, sometimes called loam

This top soil eventually grew
a garden, a pasture, an orchard,
a field of hay, a forest and a
meadow full of wildflowers

The soil, sometimes called loam,
supported a family, nourished children
and provided food, lumber, taxes and fresh
clean water for the local community

The next family that lived on
this top soil hated the land and
the soil suffered. The family did not
prosper and moved, and
the community became smaller

The new owner did not live on the land
The orchard and forest were stripped, the
garden and fields abandoned and the
buildings destroyed. The top soil remained
but now called LOAM

As a final insult Mother Earth was skinned.
The 10,000 year old top toil was scraped off,
piled up, sold and hauled away to an
urban development as loam

Currently Mother Earth is ready
to begin the long slow process
of making top soil again, but not here, this
area is now a parking area covered with
asphalt.

Things that Move

My life has many
Small things that
Move around in
Mysterious ways

Eyeglasses on
The night stand
End up in bed
Or on my head

My false teeth
Left to soak
Back in my
Mouth at dawn

Tools stored neatly
In the garden
One always goes
To the back door

Car keys kept in
Right hip pocket
Found in the left
Under my wallet

Paired stockings
Kept in drawers
Changing partners
All night long

Do you have things
That move around
Or is your life
Settled and secure?

Who is keeping track?

This week I watched
ten acres of green grass,
wildflowers, shrubs, trees
and a vernal pool disappear
They are building a shopping area

In a few days the
bulldozers stripped one
of my favorite roadside
wildlife viewing areas
No more bluebirds, deer,
ducks or monarch butterflies

In these days of increasing
air pollution problems
my loss seems minor
compared to the loss of ten
acres of green chlorophyll-producing
vegetation

Chlorophyll is the only
working system of cleansing our
polluted air. Scientists and
engineers are busy trying to
find a technological substitute
So far none are available
and none will be free
like chlorophyll

The problem is no one knows
how much chlorophyll is needed and
no one is keeping track. We may have already
exceeded the tipping point

Maybe mother earth is
keeping track

Earth's warming temperatures,
melting glaciers, rising ocean
levels and more extreme weather
events all work toward increased
plant life containing chlorophyll

www.ingramcontent.com/pod-product-compliance
Lightning Source LLC
LaVergne TN
LVHW011209080426
835508LV00007B/686